Wicked Weather for Walking

A Passiontide Progress

— STEPHEN PLATTEN —

Sacristy
Press

Sacristy Press
PO Box 612, Durham, DH1 9HT

www.sacristy.co.uk

First published in 2021 by Sacristy Press, Durham

Sacristy Limited, registered in England
& Wales, number 7565667

British Library Cataloguing-in-Publication Data
A catalogue record for the book is
available from the British Library

ISBN 978-1-78959-191-0

*For all at Holy Trinity and St Mary,
Berwick-upon-Tweed, with thanksgiving as
fellow-pilgrims in the Christian life.*

Contents

An Obsecration before the Cross

Lord, by this sweet and saving Sign,
Defend us from our foes and thine.

Jesu, by thy woundèd feet,
Direct our path aright.

Jesu, by thy nailèd hands,
Move ours to deeds of love.

Jesu, by thy piercèd side,
Cleanse our desire.

Jesu, by thy crown of thorns,
Annihilate our pride.

Jesu, by thy silence,
Shame our complaints.

Jesu, by thy parchèd lips,
Curb our cruel speech.

Jesu, by thy closing eyes,
Look on our sin no more.

Jesu, by thy broken heart,
Knit ours to thee.

Yes, by this sweet and saving Sign,
Lord, draw us to our peace and thine.

From *Cuddesdon Office Book* (Cambridge English Classics, 1904), p. 217. The first two lines are from Richard Crashaw, *Office of the Holy Cross*.

Introduction

Intriguingly, some of the most attractive roads in England are built on a gentle curve. Nash's Regent Street in London would lose something of its elegance without its arc-like way into Piccadilly Circus; "The High" in Oxford unfolds all the way along as one travels westwards between various dreaming spires; even Gold Hill in Shaftesbury, made famous by the picture of the young lad struggling to the top with his bicycle basket full of Hovis has a great sense of romance as it spirals upwards. Part of this, of course, is that continuous unveiling of a mystery and not only for those who have never been to these places before. There is always a revelatory feeling of newness in such experiences. This is an essential part of any journey and can feel threatening as well as exciting.

Any journey, then, is likely to have its surprises—some of which will be illuminating and others dark; some bringing a sense of liberation and others feeling threatening. Which way should we go? Ought we to be pursuing challenges or seeking a comfortable pathway? I can remember once saying to a friend that I was looking forward so much to a new challenge; my friend responded that he would be happiest if he never had to face another challenge in his life! Often, we cannot know what a journey will bring or how it will turn out. Robert Frost's oft-quoted poem *The Road Not Taken* gives perhaps the best summary of such experiences:

> Two roads diverged in a wood, and I—
> I took the one less travelled by,
> And that has made all the difference.[1]

Journeys, then, often include an unpredictability, a mystery, even a series of challenges. In Lent and Holy Week, the journey is effectively that of the *Via Dolorosa* in Jerusalem. This is not one street but a collection of lanes and ginnels in old Jerusalem, which take the pilgrim past the key sites associated with the passion of Jesus. Often this journey is mirrored in churches across our world as pilgrims walk the "Stations of the Cross".

But through the centuries such experiences have been extended to take pilgrims over hundreds of miles even. Many have given up three or six months to follow the so-called *Camino*, that is, the road to Santiago in north-west Spain. In England, the ancient footpath called "Pilgrim's Way" takes the devout traveller across much of southern England to the shrine of Thomas Becket in Canterbury. Similar pathways traced their journeys to St Cuthbert's tomb in Durham Cathedral. The power of such journeying is astonishing. At the beginning of the fifteenth century, Margery Kempe, daughter of a three-times Mayor of King's Lynn, made her way on separate occasions to the shrine of St Brigitte in Sweden, to that of St Francis in Assisi, to Rome and even to the Holy Land; all this was amazing remembering the exigences of travel in those far off days. Indeed, the Spanish nun Egeria followed the *Via Dolorosa* as early as the fourth century.

The reflections in this small book are intended to take you, wherever you are when reading it, along a similar journey, but in the company of those who have made such journeys before, sometimes centuries before. Interwoven with the journey of Holy Week is something of the early Christian history of these islands, often itself bound up with different patterns and understandings of pilgrimage. Different destinations make their appearances along the way. These reflections can either be used one each week throughout Lent, or one each day throughout Holy Week, beginning on Palm Sunday. They can be supplemented if you would like to read more by using as a companion volume *Pilgrims*, published by Sacristy Press and written by the same author. Travel safely, or "go well" as is more frequently said in Africa. There are readings and prayers to accompany you on your way.

The beginning of the journey
Mark 11:1–10

When they were approaching Jerusalem, at Bethphage and Bethany, near the Mount of Olives, he sent two of his disciples and said to them, 'Go into the village ahead of you, and immediately as you enter it, you will find tied there a colt that has never been ridden; untie it and bring it. If anyone says to you, "Why are you doing this?" just say this, "The Lord needs it and will send it back here immediately."' They went away and found a colt tied near a door, outside in the street. As they were untying it, some of the bystanders said to them, 'What are you doing, untying the colt?' They told them what Jesus had said; and they allowed them to take it. Then they brought the colt to Jesus and threw their cloaks on it; and he sat on it. Many people spread their cloaks on the road, and others spread leafy branches that they had cut in the fields. Then those who went ahead and those who followed were shouting, 'Hosanna! Blessed is the one who comes in the name of the Lord! Blessed is the coming kingdom of our ancestor David! Hosanna in the highest heaven!'

1

Why journey?

Some years ago, a friend of mine was interviewing someone for a new post as a teacher. Aiming to be sensitive to the candidate's motives for applying for the post, he asked him: "Tell me about your journey." In reply, the candidate said that as usual when coming into town he caught the 49 bus—sometimes it was held up by traffic and that had happened today. My friend had been just that little bit too subtle in his first question, for he'd been trying to elicit from the young man something about his *life's* journey. The 49 bus took them off on rather a different road than had been intended, so to speak.

I begin there, since "journey" has become a popular metaphor for our lives—one's entire life can be seen as a pilgrimage.

Journeying then is hardly a choice, it is a fact of life. This takes us back to the very beginning of Christian patterns of pilgrimage. For increasingly it's believed that the kernel of the four Gospels themselves springs from the story of the final days of Jesus' life, the end of his journey. One scholar even speaks of Mark's Gospel, now universally believed to be the first Gospel to be written, as a passion narrative with an extended introduction. Mark is not only the earliest but the shortest of the Gospels—the passion story does indeed take up so much of it. The assumption is then, that Mark's passion, as we now know it, began as a pilgrimage around old Jerusalem with followers of Jesus—those we'd now call the first Christians—following in the footsteps of Jesus in those final days: from his entrance into the holy city on Palm Sunday, and then following the events we now remember during Holy Week and praying through them—rather like "stations of the cross". The route in Jerusalem associated with that journey is still called the *Via Dolorosa,* the way of sadness and pain.

That focus on Jesus' passion has always stayed with patterns of pilgrimage. Two rather different takes on it developed from earliest days. The pattern most familiar to us was to travel, often in company with others, to somewhere that had resonances of great holiness. So, to journey to Jerusalem itself, to Rome, Assisi (because of St Francis), Santiago de Compostela in Spain (where it was believed St James had been laid to rest), to Durham for Cuthbert, Lindisfarne for Aidan, and Canterbury for Thomas Becket. Canterbury is doubly interesting, for not only is it the destination set at the end of the ancient path known as "Pilgrim's Way" but, following Becket's murder, Henry II, who had effectively been responsible for Becket's martyrdom, made pilgrimage to Rome as a serious act of penance.

Often, however, pilgrimage was embarked upon as a "holiday", that is, pilgrims aimed to arrive at their final destination on the "Holy Day" of the local saint—so for Compostela in Spain, that meant 25 July, the feast of St James. The entire experience would lead to a deepening of the pilgrim's faith—conversations with people along the road, prayers throughout the day, pilgrim Masses on the journey, and then the final and remarkable experience of arriving in an entirely new and different place, a place where people often had never been before.

It was from this experience that the scallop shell became the sign of the pilgrim. People would travel hundreds of miles across Europe to Santiago de Compostela in north-west Spain. They would sing pilgrim songs en route; they would exchange stories of how their faith had been deepened; they would rejoice together at Mass in the great cathedral. But then they would travel another thirty kilometres to a place called Finisterra (which simply means the "end of land"), where they would pick up a scallop shell on the beach to prove that they had completed the journey.

Pilgrimage was and still is a serious business, but it's also enjoyable in almost all its associations, except perhaps on occasion when the overnight stay is more than rough! Alongside this model of pilgrimage runs a very different one, and this grew particularly out of Irish patterns of Christian life. Over on the wild Atlantic seaboard, monks would live on deserted islands in the loughs or out on tiny, jagged rock outcrops at the edge of the ocean. Living an austere and ascetic life, rather like the fourth-century Egyptian "Desert Fathers"—St Anthony and others—they might be hermits or live in tiny monasteries, almost always in small groups, and known as sketes or skelligs. The intense life of prayer would convince them that God had called them to be pilgrims for Christ. They would set off in tiny coracles or cobles and be carried to they knew not where.

The Voyage of St Brendan is an ancient mixture of truth and legend, telling the tale of such a pilgrim with his small group of brethren. Columba chancing his life in setting out for Iona is perhaps the story we know best. But there was also St Fursey who set off from Lough Corrib, south of Donegal, not knowing where he would land. The wind and currents brought him to Burgh Castle, a deserted Roman fortress in Norfolk from whence he became one of the two great missionaries to bring the Gospel to East Anglia. It was a sort of martyrdom—in the process, many doubtless lost their lives or rather, gave them for Christ.

Either the beginning of Lent or Palm Sunday could hardly be a better time to begin a pilgrimage and to use it to deepen our prayer. The Gospel passage from Mark 11, which preceded these words, has all the marks of pilgrimage. Jesus' destination is the temple, the ultimate place of prayer with the "holy of holies" at its heart. There is also a clear sense of excitement and mystery about it. How will it all turn out? There is too a sense of foreboding: Jesus knows that he must follow the will of the Father, since as the Incarnate Son he has a destiny. The whole of this unfolding story is about that very destiny. There is an extraordinary tension in the air. The climax of the entire Gospel is soon to become clear, but this entry into Jerusalem remains a moment of glory and exultation—Jesus is heralded and greeted as a king. Branches fall into the road before him—people shout *Hosanna* and *Blessed is he who comes in God's name.* The feeling of irony could hardly be greater; how can one make sense of a king riding on a donkey? (Anyone who has organized a Palm Sunday procession knows the unpredictability of donkeys in every sense!)

So, here is a moment often acted out in the liturgy, which captures the very essence of pilgrimage—the final outcome remains a mystery; no pilgrimage is a foregone conclusion. Huge reserves of energy are an essential ingredient—think of those hundreds of miles in all weathers, think of a journey and a road you've never taken before.

A hundred years ago, the American writer Robert Frost, one of the best-loved nature poets, wrote these brief telling verses, set in this case in the depths of winter:

> Whose woods these are I think I know.
> His house is in the village though;
> He will not see me stopping here
> To watch his woods fill up with snow.

My little horse must think it queer
To stop without a farmhouse near
Between the woods and frozen lake
The darkest evening of the year.

He gives his harness bells a shake
To ask if there is some mistake.
The only other sound's the sweep
Of easy wind and downy flake.

The woods are lovely, dark and deep,
But I have promises to keep,
And miles to go before I sleep,
And miles to go before I sleep.[2]

In those lines, so much of what this journey is about, Jesus' journey and pilgrimage to cross and resurrection, are captured. The darkest night of the year—notice the darkness which Mark describes, covering the whole land, at the crucifixion. And Jesus too has promises to keep—following his Father's will even unto the end. But what makes this week's journey so much more powerful is that the end of the journey will not come swiftly, and certainly not easily. Jesus too has miles to go before he sleeps, and it will be the sleep of death, a death as final as any death—albeit for us coloured by the promise of Easter morn. Were it not a real death, how would we make sense of the grief of the women—his mother, the other women at the tomb and of Mary Magdalen in the garden, still grief-stricken at Easter's dawn?

Soon after one of my earliest essays was published, a reader of the journal wrote a quizzical letter to the editor saying that my article left one in the air; it suggested that "to travel hopefully is better than to arrive"—a well-known phrase! But part of pilgrimage is about just that: travelling hopefully is at its heart, never pre-empting our arrival. It will, of course, be that final arrival that crowns the journey—but that is to leap ahead. First we must travel an increasingly dark path with Jesus.

A prayer at the beginning of our journey

O Christ the King of glory,
who entered Jerusalem in humility
to be made perfect through suffering and death:
Enter into our hearts, we pray,
that we may offer ourselves entirely to you.
Grant us, as your faithful followers,
blessed by your coming among us,
and for whom palm branches were
    spread in your path,
to be ready to lay at your feet all we have and are,
and continually to give ourselves to you,
who comes in the name of the Lord. Amen.

An encounter in the temple
Mark 11:15–19

Then they came to Jerusalem. And he entered the temple and began to drive out those who were selling and those who were buying in the temple, and he overturned the tables of the money-changers and the seats of those who sold doves; and he would not allow anyone to carry anything through the temple. He was teaching and saying, 'Is it not written, "My house shall be called a house of prayer for all the nations"? But you have made it a den of robbers.'

And when the chief priests and the scribes heard it, they kept looking for a way to kill him; for they were afraid of him, because the whole crowd was spellbound by his teaching. And when evening came, Jesus and his disciples went out of the city.

2

Twin roots

You can still find many pictures of the Jarrow March of October 1936. Two hundred unemployed men set out for London and presented a petition at Westminster asking the government to direct new industry to the town, following the closure of Palmer's shipyard. It was a sort of "pilgrimage of the poor". Setting out on a testing journey, those who took part aimed at prospering new life for themselves and all people of working age in the town. The march's immediate results were few, but it has taken its place as an emblematic event in the life of the nation.

Alongside that, let me place one more pilgrimage from Jarrow, one which took place just a little earlier on, I say with a twinkle in my eye! Three years ago, at the British Library in London, there was a fascinating exhibition of artefacts, titled simply *Anglo Saxon Kingdoms*. Perhaps the jewel in the crown of the exhibits was the huge *Codex Amiatinus,* the oldest complete translation of the Bible in the Latin Vulgate version. In 716 the abbot of the Jarrow-Wearmouth monastery, Bede's monastery, one Coelfrith, set out to deliver it to the See of Peter, to Pope Gregory II, in Rome. This was a true pilgrimage of self-sacrifice, since Coelfrith died on the way, and his fellow monks would continue it on to Rome. The London exhibition was an amazing moment, for it was the first time that the Codex had returned to England since being completed and taken to Rome 1,300 years ago.

This reminds us of the significance of the ancient kingdom of Northumbria, both in the religious and also, ultimately, in the cultural and even political history of England. It was to be an indefatigable culture, as we can see from the courage of those Jarrow marchers some 1,300 years on. As we continue to celebrate this culture, it is easy to assume that this was the first that these islands ever knew of the Christian message, but that would be to make a serious error, for archaeological evidence alone tells us that there was Christian observance, at least in pockets, throughout Roman Britain. So, in an archaeological dig of 2009, at Binchester in County Durham, a third-century ring was found which clearly predates the accession of the Emperor Constantine, proclaimed from York in 306. The ring has Christian symbols etched into it—two fish hanging from an anchor.

Now we don't know precisely when the Christian narrative first entered these islands—it looks to have been either in the late third or early fourth century. So, it's likely that some legionnaires on Hadrian's Wall will have been Christian believers. St Alban, to whom we shall return later on, was probably martyred c. 250. The church of St Martin in Canterbury was almost certainly there as early as 380 and survives to this day. St Michael, Cornhill, where I served for three years as Rector, was built directly over the temple site in the Roman city of Londinium, where previously the Roman Emperor had been worshipped. Moving further north to Lincoln, in the 1970s, the ancient church of St Paul-in-the-Bail was discovered by accident. Again, that dated back to the late fourth century. Earlier still in 314, three bishops from London, Lincoln and York had made pilgrimage, so to speak, to the Council of Arles in Provence, convened by Constantine himself.

So, the mission-pilgrimages from Ireland and from Rome in the seventh century were effectively a second wave of mission. Indeed, relations with the surviving "British" church, as the earlier Christian community is known, were not always positive. There was a stand-off between Augustine of Canterbury and the British bishops on the banks of the River Severn near Bristol. The event is immortalized in the name of the place: Aust, after Augustine!

But two more sets of pilgrims would come, as we've already seen, and there are two parts of England where we can trace this most easily. First, in East Anglia. In the first chapter, we encountered Fursey, coming all the way from the far west of Ireland and being beached on the shore near Great Yarmouth. There he set up a monastery, built of timber, in the lee of the ruined Roman fort at Burgh Castle. Post holes there, from Fursey's monastery, have been investigated by archaeologists. But Fursey was not the only foreign pilgrim. In the second wave of pilgrim missionaries from Rome came a party led by St Felix, after whom Felixstowe was later named. He came to the kingdom of Raedwald, whom we believe to have been interred in the ship burial at Sutton Hoo. So significant was Felix, that when Herbert de Losinga built his great cathedral at Norwich in 1096, he commissioned a stone relief of Felix to be placed over the door from his palace into the cathedral—for Herbert was Felix's lineal successor. Moreover, Herbert was another pilgrim for penitence; he travelled to Rome to make penance for the sin of simony—he had *bought* the rights to the bishopric and that was a grave sin!

In Northumberland, there were also two missions. One of these was an Irish mission led by Aidan—King Oswald had asked Iona to send missionaries. The first monk, one Corman, was a disaster so Aidan was sent in his stead; even with Aidan, Oswald needed an interpreter, for Aidan spoke an entirely different language. As with East Anglia, Rome also sent missionaries, the most famous being Paulinus who baptized many in the River Glen, just below Yeavering, only fifteen miles or so from modern Berwick-upon-Tweed. The toughness of pilgrimage and clear tensions with the establishment have been hinted at all along. The patronage of monarchs was often vital—Oswald in Northumbria, Ethelbert in Kent. But others like Raedwald in East Anglia and Penda in the Welsh Marches were Pagan and often violently opposed to Christian mission. Penda, for example, was responsible for King Oswald's (later *Saint* Oswald's) death at the Battle of Maserfield, probably modern-day Oswestry. Oswald's body was mutilated but his remains were buried first in Bardney Abbey in Lincolnshire, and then his head was finally interred in Durham Cathedral. Like Cuthbert, even his remains moved in semi-pilgrimage.

These tensions and clashes with the establishment bring us directly back to Holy Week, and the Gospel passage from Mark, the "Cleansing of the Temple". It is the only occasion in which we see Jesus showing pronounced anger. It may well be one within that pattern of events that ultimately brought Jesus to his death. What is fairly clear from the New Testament narrative is that, on occasion after occasion, Jesus fell foul of the Jewish religious authorities. It is perhaps most apparent in Mark's very terse Gospel narrative. Even in Chapter 1, we are told Jesus could no longer go anywhere openly; in Chapter 2 the Pharisees challenge him, and early in Chapter 3 we read that "The Pharisees went out and immediately conspired with the Herodians against him, how to destroy him" (v. 6).

The most likely explanation of why Jesus met his fate is twofold. First, as just noted, Jesus had shown himself to be no friend of the Jewish religious establishment. The grain of his teaching ran against the entire pattern then in existence. The dangers for Jesus were exacerbated by the High Priesthood being both professional and inherited—it was a family affair. Jesus' teaching and popularity ran counter to all their hopes and fears. The Roman authorities, however, were mainly concerned with order and seeking a quiet life—the threat to them was that by antagonizing the priestly establishment, Jesus would encourage instability and even rebellion. If this was the case, then the incident in the temple would be highly inflammatory in such a key location. All the Gospel writers, bar John, place the temple cleansing immediately before Jesus' passion. The scene is set then. The thunderclouds are gathering.

From now on follows an inexorable pilgrimage of terror and fear. The reactions of the disciples, including Peter's cowardly response, which we encounter later in the story, indicate how perilous things will become. Happily, in our own world, pilgrimage is hardly likely to augur a dangerous journey. Nonetheless, anyone embarking upon such a journey cannot know what challenges the future might bring. Might it change my life radically?

W. H. Auden wrote a quirky, amusing, but penetrating poem which touches on the impact of love and the transformation of life. Here are just a few lines:

When it comes, will it come without warning
Just as I'm picking my nose?
Will it knock on my door in the morning,
Or tread in the bus on my toes?

Will it come like a change in the weather?
Will its greeting be courteous or rough?
Will it alter my life altogether?
O tell me the truth about love.[3]

Of course, the first followers of Jesus, in that portentous final week of his life, did indeed have their lives "changed altogether". For them, in different ways, the pilgrimage would refashion their lives, and not without pain, as the example of Peter shows in his denial and grief.

A prayer in time of conflict or danger

O Lord, in your arms I am safe
As long as you hold me, I feel no fear;
If ever you should let me go
All hope would fall from me.
I know nothing of what my future promises
But I rest all my trust in you.
Amen.

Mark 12:1–11

Then he began to speak to them in parables. 'A man planted a vineyard, put a fence around it, dug a pit for the wine press, and built a watchtower; then he leased it to tenants and went to another country. When the season came, he sent a slave to the tenants to collect from them his share of the produce of the vineyard. But they seized him, and beat him, and sent him away empty-handed. And again he sent another slave to them; this one they beat over the head and insulted. Then he sent another, and that one they killed. And so it was with many others; some they beat, and others they killed. He had still one other, a beloved son. Finally he sent him to them, saying, "They will respect my son." But those tenants said to one another, "This is the heir; come, let us kill him, and the inheritance will be ours." So they seized him, killed him, and threw him out of the vineyard. What then will the owner of the vineyard do? He will come and destroy the tenants and give the vineyard to others. Have you not read this scripture:

> "The stone that the builders rejected
> has become the cornerstone;
> this was the Lord's doing,
> and it is amazing in our eyes"?'

3

Columba and Aidan

Quite a long while ago now, I was approached to see if I would take part in a thing called the Duke of Edinburgh's Commonwealth Conference. It was a sort of upmarket preparatory course, should you happen to go on to a more senior post. Our two sons always scoffed: "Oh, Dad's just off to his Duke of Edinburgh's Award Scheme." This was to puncture any hint of pomposity, to keep me in my place! During those ten days of the conference, we heard several distinguished speakers, but, without a doubt, the most impressive and attractive was John Smith, soon to become Leader of Her Majesty's Opposition. Fewer than five years later he was dead. Now I begin there because, just two weeks after his death, he was buried amongst kings—Scottish and Norse—on the Inner Hebridean Isle of Iona.

Iona, of course, gained its prestige from Columba, who made his missionary pilgrimage from Letterkenny, near Donegal, in 563. Columba was an O'Neill, the family of the High King of Ireland. Like John Smith,

Columba was no stranger to politics, but more than that he knew violence and danger—he'd been party to the defeat of another O'Neill, all in the cause of the advance against Paganism.

Columba brought with him a pattern of Christian devotion distinctively different from those represented by Augustine of Canterbury. Ireland inherited a landscape and culture very different from most of mainland Europe and even much of England. There were no towns or cities and so the pattern that developed was one of monasteries or, to use the Anglo-Saxon term, "minsters". There would be a central church, with a community of prayer, from which missionaries would go out into the surrounding countryside. It would not be easy. The countryside was boggy, desolate and wild, and the Pagans were by no means friendly! But this way of operating was effective, and a characteristic culture grew. It's often referred to as "Celtic", but that's confusing in itself, for very often Celts were fairly aggressive Pagans. They had arrived in these islands well before the Roman invasion and the Britons and Irish were part of this ethnic group. Their origins can be traced back all the way across Europe; even in Georgia in the Caucasus, artefacts and symbolism similar to those found here are also often discovered.

So, the pattern of pilgrimage they brought is more accurately described as Irish. Some of the great Christian centres in Ireland had formerly hosted Pagan shrines— Kildare, for example, means "church of the oak", a grove, remembering an earlier Pagan form of worship; Armagh hosted Druid worship before it became St Patrick's primary sanctuary. We easily forget how late on Paganism survived even in mainland Europe. Remembering this, David Bentley Hart, in his *Atheist Delusions*, has illustrated just how *radical* the Gospel of Christ was. Paganism was a perfectly sane religion in most of its forms, but it was inherently sad—it offered not one ounce of hope.[4]

Interestingly, in the light of this, Pope Gregory the Great, who had sent Augustine on his way to England, had given his monks wise advice—do not destroy Pagan sites. Instead, subtly introduce the native population to the Gospel and those sites can become Christianized. Therefore, the easy juxtaposition of Irish (or popularly now, Celtic) and Roman patterns is unhelpful and inaccurate. Patrick, for example, who brought the faith to Ireland from Wales, was a thoroughly Roman Christian; indeed, the roots of the conversion of Ireland ultimately stemmed from mainland continental Europe and perforce, Rome—another good reason for avoiding the Celtic stereotype.

From Iona, then, issued a different flavour of Christian witness from that which came directly from Rome. The monks there kept Easter on a slightly different date, the monks' tonsures were different, the poetry was distinct, the monasteries and worship contrasted with mainland Europe, and Columba was not living there alone! In the first chapter, I mentioned Fursey. Then too, there is all that stands behind the book describing the legendary *Voyage of St Brendan*. Here is a legend of a seaborne pilgrim gallantly risking his life for the message of the Christian Gospel. Then also there is the witness of Columbanus. He came from south-east Ireland, moved to Ulster and from there took to the seas, risking life and limb. He travelled through Gaul as a missionary and ultimately set up his monastery at Bobbio near Piacenza in north-west Italy.

All this also sets the background for ancient Northumbria. For into this part of Britain came those two distinct strands, the Irish and the Roman. Northumbria was originally two kingdoms—Deira from the Humber to the Tees, and Bernicia from the Tees to Edinburgh. Indeed, Northumbria did not lose Lothian until the turn of the first millennium—instead of Scottish independence, perhaps *the English* should be reclaiming Lothian! Into this world, then, in the early seventh century came two distinct missionary pilgrimages, for Oswald had invited Iona to send down pilgrim missionaries to his kingdom. One Corman was sent, a severe and austere monk who, as we might now say, did the Christian Gospel no favours! So counter-effective was he, that he was despatched back to the Inner Hebrides and Aidan was sent in his place. Aidan was a very different character. He chose the tidal island of Lindisfarne for his base. Bizarre as it might seem, there was method in Aidan's madness. The island was perfect for the pattern of monastic silence and retreat, important in the Irish mission. But not only that, it was just across the water from Bamburgh, the site of the king's palace and of royal power. Bede writes of Aidan and of Lindisfarne:

> As the tide ebbs and flows, this place is surrounded by sea, twice a day, like an island, and twice a day the sand dries and joins it to the mainland. The king always listened humbly and readily to Aidan's advice and diligently set himself to establish and extend the Church of Christ throughout his kingdom.[5]

But, not so far away, at Yeavering, stood another royal palace. Here would come another pilgrim missionary, Paulinus, this time part of the contingent sent out from the monastery of San Gregorio, on the Caelian hill in Rome, by Pope Gregory the Great. On the roadside there is a memorial marking the place and we shall revisit Ad Gefrin, as it's called, in a later chapter.

Where does this leave us on that other pilgrimage, Jesus' final journey through Jerusalem in this Holy Week, often simply called the Great Week? Well, we set out this time by reading that terrifying story of the tenants in the vineyard. It's both telling and puzzling. It's telling since it rings true to the baser instincts of our humanity. The tenants, consumed with greed and avarice, care not what it costs in human lives to better their lot. They kill the owner's servants and then, with a curious turn in the tale, when he sends his son they slay him too. It's hard to work out the logic of that, unless it's the master himself who will be next for the executioner's axe. The point of the parable is, of course, to point forward, at this advanced stage in Mark's Gospel, toward the fate of Jesus. The journey is increasingly threatening, even before we arrive at the story of Gethsemane, the arrest, the trial and the crucifixion. The mood in the air is dark. That final quotation from Psalm 118 adds a cruel twist of irony:

> The stone that the builders rejected
>   has become the cornerstone;
> this was the Lord's doing,
>   and it is amazing in our eyes.

Mark is once again relentlessly reminding his readers of the inevitability of Jesus' destiny. For, for all that Jesus' teaching and manner of life (and death, of course) point to the fulfilment of our true humanity, we cannot readily absorb it. As T. S. Eliot famously noted, "Mankind cannot bear too much reality". The very life for which Jesus stood threatened the status quo. He had to go! Jews and Romans were agreed on that.

One inheritance passed down to us from the Irish pilgrim missionaries is the "breastplate prayer", prayers which promise God's constancy, whatever the odds. The most famous in its modern form is, of course, St Patrick's Breastplate. This verse of that prayer captures both the struggle and perils of pilgrimage, the now familiar images of the sea and some of the challenges of pilgrims' journeys, but also the constancy of God:

> I bind unto myself today
> the virtues of the star-lit heaven,
> the glorious sun's life-giving ray,
> the whiteness of the moon at even;
> the flashing of the lightning free,
> the whirling wind's tempestuous shocks,
> the stable Earth, the deep salt sea
> around the old eternal rocks.

As well as this you'll remember, perhaps, this final verse of a lyrical hymn based on that same breastplate tradition:

> High King of heaven, thou heaven's bright Sun,
> O grant me its joys after victory is won;
> Great Heart of my own heart, whatever befall,
> Still be thou my vision, O Ruler of all.

In all this, and in both of the traditions of pilgrimage, there is a call to courage and strength. It is not characterized in a Stoic defiance despite all. It is far more positive than that. Jesus approaches his death with his heart firmly there at the heart of God. It is that which gives credence to our talk of resurrection.

A prayer for protection

The compassing of God be on thee,
The compassing of the God of life.

The compassing of Christ be on thee,
The compassing of the Christ of love.

The compassing of the Spirit be on thee,
The compassing of the Spirit of Grace.

The compassing of the Three be on thee,
The compassing of the Three preserve thee,
The compassing of the Three preserve thee. Amen.

A Betrayer Amongst Us
Mark 14:17–21

When it was evening, [Jesus] came with the twelve. And when they had taken their places and were eating, Jesus said, 'Truly I tell you, one of you will betray me, one who is eating with me.' They began to be distressed and to say to him one after another, 'Surely, not I?' He said to them, 'It is one of the twelve, one who is dipping bread into the bowl with me. For the Son of Man goes as it is written of him, but woe to that one by whom the Son of Man is betrayed! It would have been better for that one not to have been born.'

4

Imperial mission

Quintin Hogg, alias Lord Hailsham, and later still, Lord Hailsham of St Marylebone, was one of the more colourful of British politicians in the twentieth century. A showman, famous for ringing a handbell at a Conservative Party Conference, and then a candidate for the leadership when Sir Alec Douglas-Home was elected, he was a devout Anglican. Hogg is interesting for us at this point, for two rather different reasons. First, he is one of just a very few people who have declared they came to faith purely through the power of reason. Hogg was learned and clever, so one could, I suppose, call him an "intellectual pilgrim". He tells of his conversion in one of his two autobiographies. Yes, he wrote two—he was not lacking in self-esteem!

That brings us to our second point of interest at this stage, for he called his second memoir simply *A Sparrow's Flight*. Those words come from a short episode in Bede's amazing history of the Church in these islands. If you've never seen that history, it's a surprisingly readable book

for something first published some 1,400 years ago. The
Penguin Classic is as good an edition as any, not that
Bede would have known it to check on its accuracy!
But we digress. Here is the passage from which Hogg
gleaned his book title. It is set in the royal palace of
Edwin, King of Northumbria. St Paulinus, the Roman
pilgrim-missionary bishop is there. One of his party
responds to a speech by Coifi, the chief priest of the
local Pagan religion:

> Your majesty, when we compare the present life
> of man on earth with that time of which we have
> no knowledge, it seems to me like the swift flight
> of a single sparrow through the banqueting hall
> where you are sitting at dinner . . . this sparrow
> flies swiftly in through one door of the hall, and
> out through another . . . what went before this
> life or of what follows we know nothing.[6]

All this, we believe, happened in the palace at Ad
Gefrin, mentioned earlier, which lay just below
Yeavering Bell near Kirknewton, in the very far north
of Northumberland. Aethelburh, Edwin's wife, had
brought Paulinus to Northumbria—Paulinus was one
of that second group of pilgrims sent by Pope Gregory
the Great to spread the Gospel here in England. He
became the first bishop of York, but on King Edwin's
defeat and death in battle, he fled south to Rochester

. . . courage was not the strongest card of these early Roman pilgrims!

This episode introduces us to what I call the "imperial mission", that is the mission sent direct from Rome by Pope Gregory the Great. As we've noted, these pilgrims came in two waves: first Augustine came to convert the Kentish court, arriving in 597; Paulinus' contingent arrived just four years later, in 601.

Augustine made his way slowly up through Italy and then stopped for a time first on the Îles de Lérins, just off the coast at Cannes, and then again at Autun in Burgundy. He liked southern France—the climate was good, and the natives were friendly! Bede notes:

> Having undertaken this far . . . and progressed
> a short distance on their journey, they became
> afraid, and began to consider returning home.
> For they were appalled at the idea of going to a
> barbarous, fierce and pagan nation, of whose
> very language they were ignorant.[7]

Like Paulinus, Augustine was not of a heroic breed, and he liked his creature comforts—for him it was Claridge's or the Ritz, not the local motel! Nonetheless, ultimately Gregory the Great's advance party was effective. There is plenty of evidence of its impact in Canterbury itself. They prayed first in the ancient Romano-British church of St Martin. But then they went on to build a Benedictine monastery—the remains of its twelfth-century successor are still there for all to see. They built too the first Saxon cathedral where Augustine would be the first bishop. Indeed, about twenty-five years ago, when the nave of Canterbury Cathedral was repaved, the foundations of the first small Anglo-Saxon cathedral were discovered at the western end of the north nave aisle. This was the church of Gregory's advance party under Augustine.

Gregory took great pains to prepare his missionary pilgrims. He was a noted moral theologian and in his *Pastoral Rule* he wrote of bishops:

> No art can be taught unless it is first learned by intense meditation; But the care of souls is of all arts the greatest; so you may judge the temerity of those who assume office without preparation.

Augustine does not seem to have imbibed this to the full. At an earlier stage, I mentioned his treatment of the Welsh bishops at Aust on the River Severn. Augustine himself noted, as Bede tells us:

> . . . if they refused to accept peace with fellow-Christians, they would be forced to accept war at the hands of enemies; and if they refused to preach to the English the way of life, they would eventually suffer at their hands the penalty of death.[8]

This was a sorry tale and hardly reflected Gregory's teaching. But the Roman imperial mission knew what its real title deeds were, and successive imperial pilgrims achieved much for the cause of Christ. So, later, it was Theodore of Tarsus, coming from the city of Paul's birth in Asia Minor, who would, as Archbishop of Canterbury, begin to establish the diocesan and parochial pattern that ensured every part of God's acre would fall within the care of the ministry of Christ's Church and which continues to this day.

Now, we've come a long way from Quintin Hogg and the sparrow's flight at Ad Gefrin, but both there and Lindisfarne-Bamburgh crystallize the patterns of pilgrimage which brought the faith to these islands. Paulinus, as part of the imperial mission, was to Edwin what Aidan and the Irish mission were to Oswald.

In both cases too, we have seen the pressures upon them, for Christian pilgrims had never journeyed outside into a wider world. The dangers which those early monks and monarchs experienced meant that *loyalty* and *betrayals* were all part of the challenges they faced.

Those words, loyalty and betrayal, take us to the heart of where we have arrived at in this Great Week, for let me remind you of the Gospel passage set out at the start of this reflection:

> Jesus said, 'Truly I tell you, one of you will betray me, one who is eating with me.'

Those are ominous and unforgettable words, and they touch the heart of human relationship and trust. Let us set it in a contemporary context. Just six years ago, Ben Macintyre published a most powerful and readable book, focused upon the spy Kim Philby. Burgess and Maclean had disappeared in 1951, when they knew they'd been rumbled, but even then it was clear there had been a third man. It was not until twelve years later that Philby himself disappeared from Beirut, again having finally been rumbled. Macintyre's book shows how charming and attractive Philby could be, and how he had nurtured loyalty using his powerful gift of friendship. Even Nicholas Elliott, the MI6 man charged with finding the third man, could not believe that Philby was the culprit right up to the moment it was all uncovered—hence the title of the book, *A Spy Among Friends*.[9]

This brings us into direct encounter with Judas Iscariot. That Marcan text says tersely of the betrayer: "It is one of the twelve, one who is dipping bread into the bowl with me." In other words, this traitor is the closest of friends, of companions, for that's what "companion" means, of course—those who break bread together. Once Philby had been identified as the third man, it became clear how he had been responsible for the deaths of so many others: British agents betrayed to their death, and others caught up in what we rather coldly describe as collateral damage. So too with Judas. He is the final agent of Jesus' death, the last piece in the menacing jigsaw.

As Holy Week unfolds, it emerges as a story of the human condition. So many of the actions and reactions are part and parcel of our compromised humanity. In some ways, the events of that day in Holy Week, often referred to as Spy Wednesday, take us to the heart. For they demonstrate a lethal abandonment of trust, and without trust it is hard to see how any society can survive. It is because I believe in what my fellow human beings tell me that any community or society can work and prosper. So it's all the more terrifying when a close friend dispenses with loyalty and trust. Playwright John Galsworthy explored this in his powerful 1920s drama *Loyalties*. In Jesus, we see humanity raised to divinity, such is his *trust*. Jesus' *trustworthiness* is indistinguishable from the divinity of the Father, such is the substance of Incarnation. Jesus' pilgrimage is by no means over. Judas' treachery catapults us into a sequel which is played out over the next three days, in what has become known as Holy Week—those three days are described as the Triduum. But, tonight, the sky is as black as one can imagine it could ever be.

A prayer following betrayal

O Lamb of God,
who with guileless lips
didst gently touch those that were full of deceit:
Receive us, thy weak and unfaithful friends,
with like forbearance,
and by the very kiss of thy pardon
    convict us of our sin;
who livest and reignest with
the Father and the Holy Spirit,
one God, world without end.
Amen.

Peter's Denial Foretold
Mark 14:22–42

While they were eating, he took a loaf of bread, and after blessing it he broke it, gave it to them, and said, 'Take; this is my body.' Then he took a cup, and after giving thanks he gave it to them, and all of them drank from it. He said to them, 'This is my blood of the covenant, which is poured out for many. Truly I tell you, I will never again drink of the fruit of the vine until that day when I drink it new in the kingdom of God.'

When they had sung the hymn, they went out to the Mount of Olives. And Jesus said to them, 'You will all become deserters; for it is written,

> "I will strike the shepherd,
>   and the sheep will be scattered."

But after I am raised up, I will go before you to Galilee.' Peter said to him, 'Even though all become deserters, I will not.' Jesus said to him, 'Truly I tell you, this day, this very night, before the cock crows twice, you will deny me three times.' But he said vehemently, 'Even though I must die with you, I will not deny you.' And all of them said the same.

They went to a place called Gethsemane; and he said to his disciples, 'Sit here while I pray.' He took with him Peter and James and John, and began to be distressed and agitated. And he said to them, 'I am deeply grieved, even to death; remain here, and keep awake.' And going a little farther, he threw himself on the ground and prayed that, if it were possible, the hour might pass from him. He said, 'Abba, Father, for you all things are possible; remove this cup from me; yet, not what I want, but what you want.' He came and found them sleeping; and he said to Peter, 'Simon, are you asleep? Could you not keep awake one hour? Keep awake and pray that you may not come into the time of trial; the spirit indeed is willing, but the flesh is weak.' And again he went away and prayed, saying the same words. And once more he came and found them sleeping, for their eyes were very heavy; and they did not know what to say to him. He came a third time and said to them, 'Are you still sleeping and taking your rest? Enough! The hour has come; the Son of Man is betrayed into the hands of sinners. Get up, let us be going. See, my betrayer is at hand.'

5

Ecclesia Anglicana

Back in the last century, when I was a Canon at the cathedral in Portsmouth, alongside my responsibilities in the diocese as Director of Ordinands and Clergy and Lay training, I was also Treasurer of the cathedral and Education Canon. Amongst other things, we set up a young people's group which doubled as a social group and as training for confirmation. Each summer we would make pilgrimage. Perhaps the most exciting of these was when more than twenty-five of us boarded a large outboard motorboat and set off from nearby Camber Dock. We made our voyage all the way along the coast, only about two hundred yards out to sea, to our destination at Selsey Bill. There we beached the boat, and leapt over the prow on to the pebbles to follow in the footsteps of St Wilfrid, just 1,300 years later!

We camped in a nearby village hall, then next morning walked the nine miles to Chichester for pilgrims' prayers and a Eucharist at the cathedral, at the shrine of St Richard. But, after supper on the evening we arrived, we said Compline (Night Prayer) together, in the nearby tiny church of St Wilfrid, then at the end someone read the short poem *Eddi's Service* by Rudyard Kipling. Eddi was Wilfrid's first biographer. The first stanzas go like this:

> Eddi, priest of St. Wilfrid
> In his chapel at Manhood End,
> Ordered a midnight service
> For such as cared to attend.
>
> But the Saxons were keeping Christmas,
> And the night was stormy as well.
> Nobody came to the service,
> Though Eddi rang the bell.
>
> "Wicked weather for walking,"
> Said Eddi of Manhood End
> "But I must go on with the service
> For such as care to attend."
>
> The altar-lamps were lighted,—
> An old marsh-donkey came,
> Bold as a guest invited,
> And stared at the guttering flame.[10]

I begin with that pilgrimage and those words since they set the scene for what unfolds at this time in the journey. Those words also introduce us to Wilfrid, one of the key dramatis personae for today's story. For, having now engaged with pilgrim missionaries from Rome and from Ireland via Iona, we arrive in Whitby in North Yorkshire, where the great abbey ruins from the twelfth century still stand proud on the cliff. It was here, in the year 664, that the Northumbrian King Oswy called a key synod or council to bring together these two pilgrim streams, the Roman and the Irish. Oswy had himself been nurtured in the Irish observance, but Eanfleda, his Queen, followed the practices of Rome; so, within one household, Easter would be celebrated at different times! Alfrith, the king's son, had persuaded his father to take the bull by the horns and confront these eccentricities head on. Eccentric though they may seem, there was, however, fierce tension between the two rival patterns.

Wilfrid was the man behind the sub-text, so to speak. Brilliant, intelligent, with boundless energy and a courageous commitment to the Gospel of Christ, he was also autocratic, imperious, and ruthless in pursuit of what he believed to be the truth. On one level, the Whitby Synod was almost a local version of the Great Council of Nicaea, inasmuch as the monarch presided, with both sides presenting their cases, albeit on this occasion with a very different agenda from that at Nicaea. The host was the redoubtable Hilda, Abbess of Whitby. Hilda, originally of the Roman observance, had been taught by Paulinus, but she then learned monastic patterns from Aidan. Hilda presided over a double monastery for men and women, a pattern followed later by Gilbert of Sempringham, and the Gilbertines in Lincolnshire and elsewhere. Wilfrid was keen to place the English Church clearly within the domain of the universal primacy of Rome. Effectively, this lay at the root of the controversy; what's new, you might ask—we're still arguing about the same issues!

Rather remarkably, through the holy wisdom of Hilda and the political acuity of Oswy, the Synod not only concluded peacefully, but there was agreement. There emerged *Communion*. Out of this amazing encounter evolved something which was unique. The observances of Rome were embraced—the dating of Easter and monks' tonsures—but the local patterns, liturgies and devotions would never lose that distinctive flavour which the rich Irish inheritance brought with it. The Synod of Whitby was effectively the birthplace of what has thereafter been referred to as *Ecclesia Anglicana*—the English observance. Even by the time of the Reformation, the main liturgical observance used in England was distinctive: the Sarum Rite, which has its origins at the cathedral at Salisbury, of course, but with its ultimate roots in this joint inheritance. There was a real growing together after Whitby. Such a history is not unique—the French Gallican Rite survives, as does the Milanesian Rite in Italy.

This was a remarkable moment and on this day in Holy Week, when supremely the roots of the Eucharist in the Last Supper are honoured, the key word *Communion* or *Koinonia* (the Greek equivalent) takes centre stage. Communion, in every sense in which the word is used, is at the very heart of the Gospel. It is that solidarity with all humanity in God, for which Jesus himself prayed. Of course, it is not something we can take for granted and still, across the world, *Communion* is seriously impaired. Wilfrid was no great exemplar for facilitating communion! He was exiled twice, came under the ban of the Pope and alienated people at will. He stands in great contrast to his peace-loving and extraordinarily holy fellow-Northumbrian, Cuthbert.

Nonetheless, alongside his combative nature ran a real devotional discipline. He was a great pilgrim, as his several journeys to Rome and his exploits in England, including his mission to the South Saxons, clearly indicate. Wilfrid worked tirelessly for links with mainland Europe—he was accompanied on one Rome pilgrimage by Benedict Biscop, the Abbot of Jarrow-Wearmouth. He also led a pilgrim mission to Frisia, upon which Willibrord and Wigbert would later build; Boniface too would travel and act as pilgrim missionary to Frisia and then Germany. Martyred in Friesland, he was buried in Fulda in Hesse. Later still, in the eighth century, Alcuin of York stood in this succession. He was appointed by Charlemagne as the scholar to his court in Aachen.

As with Boniface, then, pilgrimage was not without its martyrs. This brings us back to the Gospel passage with which I began this reflection, in which Mark describes the Last Supper, traditionally seen as the birthplace of the Eucharist, followed by the prediction of Peter's denials and the time in the Garden of Gethsemane. Jesus offers up and blesses the bread and the cup and concludes:

> Truly I tell you, I will never again drink of the
> fruit of the vine until that day when I drink it
> new in the kingdom of God.

The sky darkens still further, although Jesus looks forward to that ultimate *communion* which he describes as the kingdom of God. They sing a hymn, and Peter declares his undying loyalty, provoking Jesus' sad prophecy of Peter's failure in trust, the theme we explored in our previous reflection. The walk to Gethsemane now takes us into the darkest night of all, and here Jesus prays that the Father might take this cup of suffering from him. But then, repeating the agony of his fears, he cries out to the Father:

> Father, for you all things are possible; remove
> this cup from me; yet, not what I want, but what
> you want.

It is at this point we feel perhaps most intensely the mystery of the incarnation, of God here among us in the man Jesus. There is no doubting Jesus' humanity in these deeply human cries of desolation. But alongside this runs the flakiness of the disciples—here is the ultimate test of trust in which they fail; here in this test of loyalty and resilience, they all gradually fall away, leaving Jesus in a state of final desolation, leading to his acknowledgement of his destiny. Jesus says boldly:

Are you still sleeping and taking your rest?
Enough! The hour has come; the Son of Man is
betrayed into the hands of sinners. Get up, let us
be going. See, my betrayer is at hand.

In his powerful Holy Week meditations, *A Procession of
Passion Prayers,* Eric Milner-White writes:

O Blessed Lord,
who coming to the Garden,
did, in an unspeakable agony bid your friends
to watch with you in prayer:
Waken us from the many sleeps of our little faith,
that we may share your pleading for
    the multitude of souls,
and for the finishing of the Father's will;
with whom you live and reign, in the
    unity of the Holy Spirit,
God for ever and ever.[11]

This captures both Jesus' suffering and its resonances
with our own hopes and fears, achievements and
failings. And so we come full circle to *Eddi's Service,*
and another dark evening when even the most devout
seemed to have fallen away:

The altar-lamps were lighted,—
An old marsh-donkey came,
Bold as a guest invited,
And stared at the guttering flame.

The storm beat on at the windows,
The water splashed on the floor,
And a wet yoke-weary bullock
Pushed in through the open door.

"How do I know what is greatest,
How do I know what is least?
That is my Father's business,"
Said Eddi, Wilfrid's priest.

"But—three are gathered together—
Listen to me and attend.
I bring good news my brethren!"
Said Eddi of Manhood End.[12]

That is where we are tonight on the eve of that day we still ironically call *Good Friday.* Amen.

A prayer in the garden

Lord Jesus Christ,
tempted as we are,
only without sin:
Bring us in the hour of temptation
to kneel beside you in the Garden;
and not to rise
until the struggle is past
and the choice resolved,
to do the Father's will;
for thy tender mercy's sake. Amen.

The Death of Jesus
Mark 15:21–39

They compelled a passer-by, who was coming in from the country, to carry his cross; it was Simon of Cyrene, the father of Alexander and Rufus. Then they brought Jesus to the place called Golgotha (which means the place of a skull). And they offered him wine mixed with myrrh; but he did not take it. And they crucified him, and divided his clothes among them, casting lots to decide what each should take.

It was nine o' clock in the morning when they crucified him. The inscription of the charge against him read, 'The King of the Jews.' And with him they crucified two bandits, one on his right and one on his left. Those who passed by derided him, shaking their heads and saying, 'Aha! You who would destroy the temple and build it in three days,save yourself, and come down from the cross!' In the same way the chief priests, along with the scribes, were also mocking him among themselves and saying, 'He saved others; he cannot save himself. Let the Messiah, the King of Israel, come down from the cross now, so that we may see and believe.' Those who were crucified with him also taunted him.

When it was noon, darkness came over the whole land until three in the afternoon. At three o' clock Jesus cried out with a loud voice, 'Eloi, Eloi, lema sabachthani?' which means, 'My God, my God, why have you forsaken me?' When some of the bystanders heard it, they said, 'Listen, he is calling for Elijah.' And someone ran, filled a sponge with sour wine, put it on a stick, and gave it to him to drink, saying, 'Wait, let us see whether Elijah will come to take him down.' Then Jesus gave a loud cry and breathed his last. And the curtain of the temple was torn in two, from top to bottom. Now when the centurion, who stood facing him, saw that in this way he breathed his last, he said, 'Truly this man was God's Son!'

6

Martyrdom and pilgrimage

A little while ago, I attended the book launch of a friend. Her book is no easy read! Its first sentence is just seven words long—with echoes of Good Friday and the seven last words. My friend Claire's words are:

> I write, because I'm going to die.

Of course, if we happen to be of a "book-writing disposition", any of us could write that, for we are all going to die. But Claire continues:

> I have myeloma, an incurable cancer of the blood. I can't defeat it, I have to live with it. My blood flows through every part of me, bringing me life as well as, now, the promise of death.

As you can imagine, it's a harrowing journey—she spares no punches. The book comprises letters written to a group of friends almost every week since her diagnosis, a diagnosis issuing from a perfectly routine medical. The book's title, *Miles To Go Before I Sleep*, is from Robert Frost's poem, quoted in the first of these meditations, so early on in our journey.[13]

Claire's pilgrimage has been challenging in a manner that most of us can't imagine. But the truth is that any pilgrimage can be fraught with danger, as indeed can any journey. For example, it's estimated that there are still at least one hundred bodies lying frozen on Everest, never recovered from the various expeditions. Then, remember Abbot Coelfrith setting out for Rome with that huge book, the *Codex Amiatinus*. He met his death on the way. Such perils include physical dangers posed by the landscape you cross, or of course illness, or maybe the brutality of our fellow men and women—most likely men. As another example, in the third century there was Alban. Alban was a pilgrim, inasmuch as he was a Roman soldier, stationed in England and a devout Christian. We know very little about him. Bede gives an account placing his martyrdom near the river Ver, after which was named the Roman city of Verulamium. St Alban's Abbey occupies the site of his martyrdom.

There's much to be said for Alban being England's patron saint, as our first named martyr.

Of course, not every pilgrim would forfeit her or his own life, but other challenges remained. Dewi, better known outside Wales now as David, is an example of someone living a life of challenge. Alongside his missionary work, Dewi was a courageous theologian.

A fourth-century Briton, one Pelagius, had been the source of a serious heresy. He argued that we can achieve goodness and union with God through our own efforts. It was a "bootstrap" theology and morality—try hard enough and we can all pull ourselves up by our own bootlaces! Augustine of Hippo, who we met earlier on, worked hard to defeat the spread of Pelagius' thought. He knew we can only come to God through God's "grace" going before us. Much of Dewi's life and work in Menevia (that is, St David's) challenged Pelagius' heresy. Dewi had no easy pilgrimage!

As a young lad such heroic tales always seemed to me to issue from a long-lost past, from a world and an age entirely different from our own. I've learnt better, of course. For all the differences, the twentieth century also witnessed countless horrific examples of martyrdom. Maximilian Kolbe, a Franciscan friar incarcerated in Auschwitz, heard that five men were to be executed. One cried out: "My wife and my children!" Kolbe gave himself up for execution, in place of that prisoner. Or, of course, there is the case of Dietrich Bonhoeffer. Bonhoeffer, through his friendship with our own Bishop George Bell, had been a tireless worker for peace during the Second World War. Ultimately, he was so appalled by Nazi genocide that he took part in the plot, conceived by Stauffenberg, Von Trott and others, to kill Hitler. Imprisoned first in Tegel Prison, then in Buchenwald concentration camp, he was eventually executed at Flossenbürg just over the border from Czechoslovakia, and less than two months before VE Day. One can still visit the place, as I have.

Sadly, the perils of Christian pilgrimage are still very immediate. Perhaps most tragically of all, they may have an impact on an entire community. Back in 1994, I had the responsibility of organizing a visit for the then Archbishop of Canterbury to Ireland. It was one of the most testing pieces of work in all my time working at Lambeth. Most visits required a preliminary reconnaissance trip. This time, so complex were the issues, that it took three planning visits to prepare the ground.

In the event, the most powerful and moving experience of the visit was a gathering in the Church of Ireland Synod Hall in Derry. A concert formed part of the evening. The whole event was happening early in the very first ceasefire in Ulster, the troubles having started two decades earlier. There was an extraordinary atmosphere in the Hall. The final item, which in any other situation might have appeared as almost pure sentimentality, was a duet. A young man and young woman sang words to the *Londonderry Air*, what we know better as *Danny Boy*. The tension was broken in that enormous room by many, if not all, becoming tearful. The province had not known peace for twenty-five years, and here it was now. This marked a key moment in a communal pilgrimage of hearts. That pilgrimage saw its springing point from a deadly conflict issuing from how different communities understood living the Christian Gospel.

Now, returning to antiquity, there are extraordinary parallels with the first martyrdom of which we have an eye-witness account. It is that of Polycarp, in Smyrna, modern-day Izmir, in the year AD 155. Polycarp had been arrested and was required to deny his faith. He was brought into an arena to be taunted by the crowd. The Governor did his best to persuade Polycarp to recant. He used his crier to incite the crowd to press Polycarp further:

> . . . at the crier's words the whole audience broke into wild yells of ungovernable fury 'That teacher of Asia, that destroyer of our gods!' The Governor made one further appeal, 'Revile your Christ!' Polycarp replied: Eighty and six years I have served Him and He has done me no wrong. How then can I blaspheme my King and Saviour?[14]

The example of these martyrs quite naturally brings us to this most solemn of days, which ironically we call *Good Friday*—"good" in earlier times was also used for holy, so it means *Holy Friday*.

The reading prefacing this reflection is one of which we hardly need reminding. Mark's Gospel account, as usual, is the tersest. It's the setting that's so powerful:

> When it was noon, darkness came over the whole land until three in the afternoon.

The picture is virtually that of an eclipse of the sun. Then Jesus cries out, quoting words from the beginning of the twenty-second psalm:

> 'Eloi, Eloi, lema sabachthani?' 'My God, My God, why have you forsaken me?'

The sense of desolation here is complete—this is no faked death we are about to witness. The sequel follows:

> Jesus gave a loud cry and breathed his last.

The centurion is knocked sideways by this:

> 'Truly this man was God's Son!'

Identifying with this in contemporary times may often feel difficult. What are we gazing upon? After all, even the cruellest regime today does not crucify people!

Some years ago, I read Jewish writer Elie Wiesel's remarkable but tortured account of his life in the death camps of Buchenwald and Auschwitz. The most telling moment for me during his incarceration he describes thus:

> Three gallows were erected ... the victim roll call included a small boy we'd called the 'sad eyed Angel'. Even the SS were more disturbed than usual—to hang a young boy in front of

thousands was no light matter. The three necks were placed at the same moment within nooses.

'Long live liberty!' cried the two adult victims, but the child was silent.

'Where is God? Where is He?' someone behind me asked.

With total silence throughout the camp, for more than half an hour the child hung there, struggling between life and death. Behind me, I heard the same man asking:

'Where is God now?' Then I heard a voice within *me* answer him: 'Where is He? Here He is—He is hanging here on this gallows.'[15]

This was the most testing moment of all for Wiesel's faith, and it comes from *our* world—Wiesel himself died in 2016.

He saw this moment as both God's death, and yet also, within himself, a perception of who God is. Wiesel, a Jewish commentator, captures something at the heart of our faith as Christians. Jesus crying out the words of Psalm 22 echoes through our consciousness.

In her most sensitive novel, *I Heard the Owl Call My Name,* Margaret Craven tells of a young priest who unknowingly is suffering from a fatal condition. His bishop, with acute gentleness, trains the young man as a pastor. He tells him: "Your whole life as a priest will be to prepare your people for their death."

That is where we began with Claire's book, and it's where our pilgrimage rests for the moment. We cannot escape the grim realities. We must live with them, but the pilgrimage has not ended . . . tomorrow is another day!

A prayer as Jesus is dying

O Lord, our Shepherd and Guide,
grant us to walk through the valley
   of the shadow of death,
fearing no evil, lacking nothing,
accompanied by thee,
who thyself hast passed that way,
and made it light;
and now livest and reignest
in the glory of the eternal Trinity, world without end.
Amen.

The Empty Tomb

When the sabbath was over, Mary Magdalene, and Mary the mother of James, and Salome bought spices, so that they might go and anoint him. And very early on the first day of the week, when the sun had risen, they went to the tomb. They had been saying to one another, 'Who will roll away the stone for us from the entrance to the tomb?' When they looked up, they saw that the stone, which was very large, had already been rolled back. As they entered the tomb, they saw a young man, dressed in a white robe, sitting on the right side; and they were alarmed. But he said to them, 'Do not be alarmed; you are looking for Jesus of Nazareth, who was crucified. He has been raised; he is not here. Look, there is the place they laid him. But go, tell his disciples and Peter that he is going ahead of you to Galilee; there you will see him, just as he told you.' So they went out and fled from the tomb, for terror and amazement had seized them; and they said nothing to anyone, for they were afraid.

Mark 16:1–8

7

The Easter People

Glasgow has not traditionally been seen as a romantic place, nor certainly a place endowed with outstanding natural beauty. Approach it from the south-east, however, and towering above the city are the pinnacles of the great medieval cathedral of St Mungo, founded in the year 543 by St Kentigern, often known as Mungo.

We know very little about Mungo—it is fairly likely that he was an Irish monk and not part of Ninian's earlier mission to Galloway. Counter-intuitively for us, Glasgow means Kentigern's beloved green place. But Glasgow has, of course, changed visibly in the past thirty years since it was proclaimed City of Culture in 1990. Charles Rennie Mackintosh's "House for an Art Lover", the Burrell Collection, the rediscovery of the buildings of Alexander "Greek" Thomson—all these and more have helped toward an extraordinary renaissance, or better still, a resurrection, the hope of which is, of course, what inspired Mungo to build his church.

I follow that with a different starting point which could hardly be a greater contrast, that is, the site of Ciaran's great monastery at Clonmacnoise in the very heart of Ireland. Here, in the water meadows formed by the vast meanders of the wide but sluggish River Shannon, lies one of the most holy places of Ireland. Ciaran, unlike Columba, had humble origins, as the son of a travelling carpenter from Connaught, in north-west Ireland. He came here in 544, just a year after Mungo had arrived in Glasgow, his beloved green place. The monastery became a powerhouse of holiness in Ireland, dedicated to witnessing to the resurrection of Jesus Christ. The power of place there remains as strong as ever. Columba came to Clonmacnoise on pilgrimage, before his own missionary journey to Iona.

The impact of patterns of pilgrimage on those who, over many centuries, travelled in faith should not be underestimated. Perhaps that journey which has been most formational, which has captured the heart of more than all others, is the road to Santiago de Compostela in north-west Spain. The impact of travelling the so-called *Camino* is remarkable. Sometimes people will devote three or even six months of their lives to making this journey, crossing international boundaries one after another, where necessary. Fairly recently, in a telephone conversation, a friend who has no particular connections with the Church said:

This is a crossroads moment on my life—and I've committed myself to walking the *Camino*."

The magnetism of this journey breaks all boundaries. An interesting way into it is through David Lodge's novel, *Therapy*. Lodge is one of the most accessible novelists of our day. He writes with wonderful ironic humour, but all nonetheless underpinned with serious foundations—Lodge himself is a lapsed Roman Catholic, but his writing is imbued with that inheritance of faith which goes back to his youth.

His novel *Therapy* is built around the story of a journey along the *Camino*. Without the normal religious connotations, it is effectively a tale interweaving different patterns of "resurrection" in people's lives. The events of the actual journey, the arrival and the experience of being in the thronged cathedral on the Feast of St James describe feelings palpable to the reader.

This impact is not coincidental, for much study has been carried out on the experience of pilgrimage, particularly by anthropologists—some who are believers, and some who are not. In understanding the culmination of the journey, the human experience of what they call *liminality* lies at its heart. At the end of such a journey, as you arrive at the destination, whatever and wherever it may be, you cross a new threshold. It is that experience which holds the possibility of utterly transforming one's life. It happens not simply by entering the shrine, the cathedral or whatever is your destination, but rather by the fact that when you do so, you complete the extended experience of pilgrimage. The experience of all that has happened, all the people you have met, all this journey has come to mean is over—the end is simply the liminal moment. Now you can begin to understand why those final few kilometres to Finisterra, to collect from the beach a scallop shell, is of real significance. For the believer, it is riven with a real experience of *resurrection*, of a new beginning born out of a deep and life-changing experience. Not a bad point at which to have arrived, at the end of either Lent or Holy Week.

This also draws together something of what we have been exploring and encountering throughout this journey. So, for example, the plethora of Irish Celtic-style wayside crosses bears witness to this. You'll remember that what we often simply call Celtic crosses include a nimbus, a circle around the centre of the cross. This symbolizes the sun and *resurrection;* indeed, some crosses also have a representation of the sun at the very centre, rather after the pattern of those eighteenth-century fire symbols one sees over the doors of old cottages. So, witness to resurrection is a continuing theme.

If we place that alongside one further theme, we begin to understand the reasons behind pilgrims and pilgrimage being so critical for the life of the world. That further theme is what I've called *unceasing prayer.* This picks up a pattern much loved in Eastern Orthodoxy, where a simple mantra is repeated—perhaps the *Jesus Prayer,* even in its longest version merely ten words. This focus on prayer is perfectly expressed in an amazing passage in the twelfth chapter of Paul's letter to the

Romans. The passage describes the journey of the Christian life, rather as in the *Beatitudes*. Paul writes:

> . . . be ardent in spirit, serve the Lord. Rejoice in hope, be patient in suffering, pray without ceasing . . .

It is that note of unceasing prayer that connects pilgrimage again with the Northumbrian tradition. The stories of Cuthbert particularly are woven with this strand, and such prayer binds the whole of life into an integrity. Bede writes:

> Above all else, Cuthbert was afire with heavenly love, unassumingly patient, devoted to unceasing prayer, and kindly to all who came to him for comfort.[16]

We have arrived, then, at that most glorious night when God raised Jesus. We have stayed with Mark, and it is Mark's account we read at the start of this reflection. As ever, with Mark, it's distinctive for its brevity but also its sense of mystery. The ending is one of the most remarkable conclusions anywhere in literature. The women find the tomb empty, a young man tells them that Jesus has been raised—and what is the denouement?

> . . . they went out and fled from the tomb, for terror and amazement had seized them; and

> they said nothing to anyone, for they were afraid.

It's breathtaking—how then do *we know of it*? Mark deliberately leaves us in suspense, and although he's the first ever to write of the empty tomb, he makes no attempt to describe any clumsy mechanics. The mystery remains.

But then, all is set within a far wider perspective which the Easter Vigil uniquely captures. The vigil begins in darkness, a new fire is kindled, and the Old Testament readings point to the amazing acts of God. From that new fire, the paschal candle, the Easter candle, is lit. Then comes the most ancient hymn, the Exultet, rehearsing the drama of salvation:

> This is the night, when first you saved our fathers, you freed the people of Israel from their slavery . . . this is the night when the pillar of fire destroyed the darkness of sin . . . this is the night when Jesus Christ broke the chains of death.

That same phrase is repeated again and again:

> This night will be as clear as day: it will become my light my joy . . . O Felix Culpa . . . O happy fault, that earned so great a Redeemer!

Back in the 1980s in a spirited address, Pope John Paul II coined a phrase, with its roots once again in St Augustine of Hippo. In generous words, he said: "We are the Easter People and Alleluia is our song." It's a good phrase—after all those days of penitence when "alleluia" is never sung, now it can echo from the rafters. To pick up that word used earlier—now, we as pilgrims have reached that "liminal moment", rather like stepping over the threshold of the shrine or the cathedral or wherever. We have followed in the steps of Christ's passion and death and now the world is changed, almost unrecognizable—now once again, lives will be transformed.

I have referred earlier to the great pilgrimages of 1997 which celebrated the arrival of the other Augustine on the Kent coast and also remembered the death of the blessed Columba. The climax of the latter journey was Derry, from whence Columba hailed. After a great ecumenical service of thanksgiving, we marched out of the cathedral. I'll never forget walking with the Anglican and Roman Catholic Bishops of Derry and other church leaders, behind fourteen oarsmen holding huge blades vertically above them. I have pictures of this wonderful sight. We arrived at the Quay, the bishops blessed the oarsmen, and they set out for Iona. It was a sign of resurrection and the beginning of an unending journey, a resurrection pilgrimage to the heart of God. That is exactly where we are at this, our own breathtaking moment, at which our life stands ready to be transformed.

Let us pray—and at this point our initial prayer is transformed . . .

Amen and Alleluia
We shall rest and we shall see
We shall see and we shall know
We shall know and we shall love
In our end which has no end.
Alleluia, alleluia, alleluia.

A prayer for God's Church

O God of unchangeable power and eternal light,
look favourably on your whole Church,
that wonderful and sacred mystery;
and by the tranquil operation of
    your perpetual providence
carry out the work of our salvation,
and let the whole world feel and see
that things which were cast down are being raised up,
and things which had grown old are being made new,
and from whom they took their origin,
even Jesus Christ our Lord.
Amen.

Acknowledgements

First and foremost, I would like to thank those from the parish of Holy Trinity and St Mary, Berwick-upon-Tweed, who were fellow travellers with me throughout Holy Week, 2021. Reflecting and praying together is an essential part of the Christian life. It is to the same parish that this book is dedicated.

Then I give great thanks to Canon Dennis Handley, who, as Vicar of Berwick, invited me to deliver these reflections in their original unedited form. Equal thanks are due to Sir Philip Mawer, who not only suggested that they might be published, but who with his usual generosity and precision read through the entire text to ensure accuracy and felicitous expression—any remaining inaccuracies or infelicities are entirely down to the author. Then, as ever, I am grateful to my wife Rosslie, both for putting up with me being closeted in the study for hours writing and typing, and then for looking through the texts to avoid too many hiccups before delivery. I hope that all these people will be pleased that others will now benefit from their labours.

Notes

[1] Robert Frost, *Selected Poems*, with an introduction by C. Day Lewis (Harmondsworth: Penguin, 1955), p. 78.

[2] Robert Frost, *Selected Poems*, with an introduction by C. Day Lewis (Harmondsworth: Penguin, 1955), p. 145.

[3] W. H. Auden, *Tell Me the Truth about Love* (London: Faber & Faber, 1999), p. 5; emphasis mine.

[4] David Bentley Hart, *Atheist Delusions: The Christian Revolution and Its Fashionable Enemies* (New Haven, CT: Yale University Press, 2010).

[5] Bede, *Ecclesiastical History of the English People*, tr. by Leo Sherley-Price (Hardmondsworth: Penguin, 1955), p. 147.

[6] Bede, *Ecclesiastical History of the English People*, tr. by Leo Sherley-Price (Hardmondsworth: Penguin, 1955), p. 129.

[7] Bede, *Ecclesiastical History of the English People*, tr. by Leo Sherley-Price (Hardmondsworth: Penguin, 1955), pp. 72–3.

[8] Bede, *Ecclesiastical History of the English People*, tr. by Leo Sherley-Price (Hardmondsworth: Penguin, 1955), p. 106.

[9] Ben Macintyre, *A Spy Among Friends: Kim Philby and the Great Betrayal* (London: Bloomsbury, 2015).

[10] Rudyard Kipling, *The Complete Verse* (London: Kyle Cathie Ltd., 2010), p. 412.

11 Eric Milner-White, *A Procession of Passion Prayers* (London: SPCK, 1950), p. 48.

12 Rudyard Kipling, *The Complete Verse* (London: Kyle Cathie Ltd., 2010), p. 412.

13 Claire Gilbert, *Miles to Go Before I Sleep: Letters on Hope, Death and Learning to Live* (London: Hodder & Stoughton, 2021).

14 *The Martyrdom of Polycarp XII.2, in Early Christian Writings*, translated by Maxwell Staniforth (Harmondsworth: Penguin, 1968, 1972), p. 158f.

15 Elie Wiesel, *Night* (New York: Bantam Books, 1960), pp. 75f.

16 Bede, *Ecclesiastical History of the English People*, tr. by Leo Sherley-Price (Hardmondsworth: Penguin, 1955), p. 260.